HOW TO BE A SUCCESSFUL REAL ESTATE AGENT

In An Industry Where 87% Fail

Tips, Checklists, And Stories To Help
You <u>Be The Exception!</u>

Paul Fontaine

TABLE OF CONTENTS

FOREWORD:

I started my career as a Computer Science major. I lost my first job because of September 11, and it changed the trajectory of my life and career forever. While looking for a second career - I got into Real Estate by accident. Today I find myself in the position of being the owner of Keller Williams Philadelphia – one of the largest residential brokerages in Philadelphia, closing on a billion dollars in sales and The Condo Shops - one of the top 100 Real Estate Teams in the country.

I have known Paul as a charismatic businessperson who agents look up to with respect and admiration. He has been a mentor to many and has helped elevate agents through teaching a multitude of classes – so I am confident that his content is coming from experience. What I did not know is that this book is not just relevant to new agents, but it also challenges experienced agents with interesting and seemingly common-sense questions. We can all use a Real Estate Primer at some point in our careers!

While reading this book Paul makes you realize how simple this business actually is, but how complicated we make it. If you follow simple steps and double it with discipline – being successful in Real Estate is only a matter of "when" not "if". Paul breaks down the residential real estate business into extremely easy steps.

This book provides a wide variety of related actions necessary to be successful in real estate by taking into consideration each person's individual learning experiences and catering at the level where everyone can learn from it. Understanding the concepts behind becoming successful is important – there isn't a cookie cutter answer to anything. Paul makes you think about your strengths to master your competitive advantages in order to focus and leverage them.

I love learning from leaders that have built great, steady businesses and discuss proven concepts and tactics for others to be successful. Paul has done exactly that here.

Every reader will relate to the author because the examples, experiences, and suggestions are from real life and not simply speculated. Paul digs deeper into your life to make you answer your "Big Why". Paul rightfully quotes - "If your Why doesn't make you cry, then that is not your Why!" Your passion and your why are the #1 priority that needs to exist in your life if you want to be successful in real estate or anything in life. I personally felt energized about my career again after reading this book.

There are some things that we go through in life – some good and some bad that unknowingly have such a great effect on us that they define our entire future – but we don't realize it until much later in life.

The Challenge portions in the book not only challenge you to do it, but also teach you how to do it. While following simple steps along the way, you will not even realize you have a full-blown marketing plan setup by the time you are done reading the book.

Starting a business in real estate can be daunting – but this book will get you there in baby steps, in an organized manner without you realizing how much you are getting done one section at a time. If you are looking to launch your real estate career, you will realize after reading this book that you are 95% ahead of the curve

This book is even more relevant now than ever before if you want to succeed in the Real Estate business. <u>Be the exception</u>....one step at a time.

Thank you Paul for writing this book. I wish I had access to this book when I got into the business myself. But I am glad that agents will be able to avail themselves of this resource and be on a solid path towards success after reading it.

Sincerely,

Gaurav Gambhir

PREFACE

First, the bad news. If you are a newer real estate agent, or thinking of becoming one, statistics show that only 13% of you will succeed in real estate. According to NAR (National Association of Realtors), 87% of agents fail within the first 5 years. The good news is that statistics don't matter when it comes to your will to succeed. Nothing has more control over whether you ultimately succeed than yourself. If you have a strong belief system and a hard-working passion to succeed, no statistics will bring you down. Success in real estate is a formula and I've cracked the code.

This book will help you <u>be the exception!</u> These strategies, tips, checklists and tools will help you become part of the top 13% of agents who succeed and thrive. Your only homework is to implement and "live" the words that follow.

Success is not easy but it's very much worth the effort. You need to have a strong motivation to <u>be the exception</u> and get to the top. **Your desire to succeed has to be stronger than your fear of failure.** Let me repeat that. Your desire to succeed has to be stronger than your fear of failure. While 'rejection' and 'embarrassment' are strong motivators, until you conquer your 'fear of failure' you will be a slave to all three.

The question here is whether your motivation to succeed in real estate is stronger than your desire to NOT do the things necessary for that success. Ask yourself the following questions:

- Is your desire to succeed stronger than your desire to sleep in?

- Is your desire to succeed stronger than your desire to procrastinate prospecting for business everyday?

- Is your desire to succeed stronger than your fear of picking up the phone to consistently follow up with your leads?

- Is your desire to succeed stronger than your need to stay in your comfort zone?

These types of questions are important to ask yourself before you begin, or continue, this journey. Be honest with yourself when answering these questions. If you discover one or more of your answers states your desire to succeed isn't stronger than your fear, take time to understand why that is and see if you can address the root of the fear. We'll discuss later how to dig deep with your "Why?" questions can help you in all aspects of your life and business.

It's time to overcome the pessimistic voice inside your head that feeds your fear and complacency. By reading this book and putting the concepts into action, you have the chance right now to stop allowing your negative inner voice from defining who you are and what you will achieve!

Every decision humans make comes down to two simple paths: Whether you want to go TOWARD PLEASURE or AWAY FROM PAIN. It's as simple as that. Life broken down into less than 10 words. Think of any decision you've ever made and I guarantee it can be classified into one of those two categories.

If you ever have a hard time understanding someone's reaction and behaviors, remember this rule of life and business: people are either finding pleasure or avoiding pain. Both of these paths are great ways to motivate yourself to succeed and they have to be very powerful if you want to be part of the elite 13% of exceptional agents in this industry. Talking about pleasure and pain, I found this quote while researching the book and thought it might speak directly to certain readers :). Maybe there are a few exceptions to the pain and pleasure human behavior rule after all!

In summary, you have to have a very big, emotionally driven need to succeed as a real estate agent since there will be many hurdles and barriers as you start, and build, your business. Let's begin this journey to <u>Be the Exception!</u> Use this book as your guide. It's an exciting journey and I know you can do it!

How I found my "Why"

When graduating with my degree in business I could never have imagined this happening to me. If you've never been fired, broken a front tooth and received a parking violation all on the same day then you're missing out on a lot of life lessons! I hope you can learn those lessons through this book and not have to go through them personally. To get to know me and understand where my desire to succeed comes from, here's my story.

After graduating college with a business degree, I was moving up the corporate ladder. I had a marketing degree and worked in various marketing and product development roles. I went through numerous layoffs where I was always the one they kept on while many others around me were let go.

At that time, in my youthful cocky mindset, I assumed it was because I was exceptional, but looking back, most likely, it was because I was still young and being paid a lower salary than the long time employees they were laying off. I got my MBA in the evenings working hard after work to finish in a couple years. I moved from state to state and company to company getting better and higher paying positions.

And then one day, it happened. I was the one who got laid off. It hurt me a bit and knocked me down a notch but it wasn't going to keep me down.

I then got a job at a small marketing company outside of Washington DC and within a year I was fired. I don't need to go into the reasons why and how I believe I was wrongly blamed for something, but that firing changed my life. To "add salt to the wound," I broke off the corner of my front tooth biting into a lollipop. I scheduled an urgent appointment and headed directly to my dentist. The appointment took a bit longer than expected and as I walked to my car to return home I saw the little gift the Philadelphia Parking Authority had left for me on my windshield. A sort of climactic ending to one hell of a day.

I attached almost all of my self worth to my career and the positions I held. When I got fired I said to myself "I'm Paul Fontaine. I don't get fired! Other people get fired, I don't" Again, I was still on the younger side at 30 years old and had this mindset that I was indispensable. That firing struck me at my core, I was lost and in shock.

A couple days later I had some pain in my back and a weird rash. I went to the doctor and he said I had shingles. I was 30 years old and I had a condition most common in older adults or those with impaired immune systems. The doctor was a bit baffled and said I should get an HIV test because it didn't make sense that someone so young would get shingles. I'll never forget that day. Not only was I so emotionally drained from the firing just a few days before, but also I was dealing with the intense physical pain of a shingles diagnosis and NOW I'm afraid I may have HIV! It was one of the lowest points of my life. Having said all of this, I didn't think it was probable that I had HIV but there was certainly a small % chance I could have contracted it being a sexually active 30 year old. Fortunately, I was tested and the results were negative but those couple weeks were the longest and hardest weeks of my life.

I look back now and give thanks for that day. It was one of the best things that ever happened to me. Yet, at that time, it was one of the worst things that I had ever experienced.

Ok. Let's shake that off and move on to a few months later. I got another job and moved back to Philadelphia. Within a month of being at my new job, my boss told me the position they had hired me for was no longer viable as a product line and they would not be launching it anymore. For a few months thereafter, they had me doing random company projects and at around the 6-month mark I was laid off for the second time in 2 years.

I remember that day clearly and I said to myself with so much emotion(mostly anger), "I am never working for someone ever again!" I had had enough and so it began. The fire inside me burned so strongly with conviction. I was hurt badly and burned too many times. I would do anything to never experience those feelings again.

Fast forward to the present, I'm happy to say I never looked back and it was the best decision I ever made. I don't think I would have become so successful if I hadn't experienced such painful events. The events I recollected can be, and often are, defined as failures. I would be lying if I said there weren't times while everything was happening that I didn't feel beaten down. Yet soon after, and most definitely now in my life, I look back with such gratitude that those "failures" happened to me. I learned a lot from those events and they continue to fuel my fire to this day.

I found myself in a new city alone and without family or a support system, so I was forced to increase my resilience and self-reliance. I did everything I could to succeed and you can too! That stoked that flame inside of me, feeding my passion and burning until I became "Rookie of the Year" my first year in real estate. I beat out every new Prudential Real Estate agent in the tri state region of NJ, PA and DE and sold $4.3 Million in sales my first year (and I didn't even start the year until March)!

(Here's my Rookie of the Year Award I still keep on my desk).

That's how I found my "why," now let's start working on yours. Through questions and self-reflection in Section 1 you will identify your motivations and personal passions to help ignite your inspirational fire and use it to succeed in this book. Once you find your personal passion use it to drive yourself to be the exception. Let's begin!

SECTION 1

MINDSET -
THE BIG PICTURE

Find your "Why?"

In this section we will discuss how to **Find your Fire, your Passion, and your Why!**

It's Friday night in the middle of December when it gets dark at 4:30pm. As I peer out my window, I check my outside thermometer showing a frigid 30 degrees. A bit of a snow flurry is coming down and I have a new client who wants to see a vacant house at 7:30pm. It's going to be a long 3 hours! It is too easy to say "Never mind, I'll just tell him it's sold or that I couldn't get an appointment confirmed" rather than get your butt off that warm, comfy couch and bundle up to drive into the dark and cold to show that property. It's at crucial times like this when you need to have that fire to get you off the couch.

Your passion and your why are the #1 priority that needs to exist in your life if you want to be successful in real estate or anything in life. I've seen it happen time and time again. New agents who are excited to begin with big dreams that ultimately fail because they realize it's a lot harder than on TV and often much less glamorous. If you don't have that fire within you, it's easy to fizzle out.

In Japan they have a concept called Ikigai (pronounced ick-ee-guy). It means "reason for being" and has been linked to longevity of life. Ikigai originated in Okinawa, Japan. This island has been documented having the largest population of centenarians (100+ year olds). It is believed that if you have Ikigai aka your fire and passion, you tend to live longer. The graph below shows Ikigai as the core overlapping point between what you love, what the world needs, what people pay you for and what you are great at.

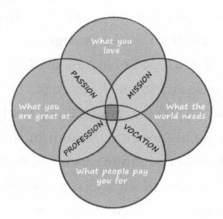

Hopefully all of that adds up to owning a real estate business if you want to be successful.

Some people have said to me "I'm not sure I have a big Why"

to which I respond "Everyone has a big Why. The question is, will that specific Why help you be successful in real estate?" As I discussed in the Preface, every action you take is either toward pleasure or away from pain. Your big Why should create a very strong emotional reaction in either direction. For me, the pain I felt from my firing and layoffs was so strong, I will do anything to keep far away from that pain again. That's a lot of what still drives me to succeed today.

CHALLENGE: Ask yourself: What do you love doing? What brings you the most joy? For example, do you feel most alive when you are helping others? Does baking excite you? Also, what are the things you never want to experience or feel? Maybe you grew up seeing your single mother struggle to make ends meet and you never want her to struggle again. Or you will never forget the embarrassment of going to school with old or dirty clothes because your parents couldn't afford to buy you new ones.

Unsure if your Why is big enough? One of my favorite motivational audio tapes, FEED YOUR MIND WITH SUCCESS, states in the portion entitled *Your Reason:* "If your Why doesn't make you cry, then that is not your Why!" The reason I love that quote is because it emphasizes the importance of having strong emotional ties to that Why. Thinking logically by using just your brain to choose a Why won't work, and if your Why doesn't bring up an emotionally, powerful connection, it's probably not strong enough to get you through the rollercoaster of owning a real estate business. And yes, you own a real estate business (more on that later).

To help you discover your Why, start asking yourself deeper and deeper questions regarding your desires. You have to ask yourself "Why?" in order to get to your Why. As a quick example:

Me: "What's your big Why to become an agent?"

Agent: "To make a lot of money."

Me: (I'd then dig deeper and ask) "Why is it important to make a lot of money?"

Agent: "So I can be rich."

Me: "Why is it important to be rich?"

Agent: " So I can feel more secure and independent". (now we are getting somewhere)

Me: "Why is it important to be more secure and independent?"

Agent: "So I never have to rely again on someone else and to show my children the importance of being independent!"

 Now that response has a strong emotional pull to it! That is a WHY important enough to overcome your insecurities and fears as you build your real estate business.

Before you continue reading, I can't emphasize enough how

crucial it is to answer this first question to help you <u>be the exception</u>. Spend time right now thinking about what is your passion and fire, your *Ikigai*, your Why and dig deep making sure you have a very strong, emotional connection.

A few years ago, a younger, and newer, agent I was speaking with said his parents worked so hard when they immigrated to this country to make a better life for him that he would do anything to make them proud. You could feel the intensity and resolve he had to become a success. If you don't have a strong enough reason to do the following things discussed in this book, you just won't do them and you'll join the 87% of past agents who had high hopes and ended up failing to live up to their dreams.

CHALLENGE: Why do you NEED to be a successful real estate agent? Before reading on, write down your WHY. No, seriously, stop reading and spend 15-30+ minutes thinking, writing down, brainstorming, digging deep and asking the important "whys?" to get to your emotional trigger.

Just do it! Don't get bogged down in logistics.

Did you do your homework? Excited about your passion and your WHY? Ok, let's move ahead.

When I first started in real estate, I had an amazing Broker and friend named May Acker and she would often say

'Everyday we wake up unemployed! Go out and find business." I think of that statement often and it reminds me of Nike's famous slogan "Just Do It."

I've always been a huge fan of the "Just Do It" advertising campaign. Interesting tidbit on the origin of the slogan. Dan Weiden, who co-founded Weiden+ Kennedy advertising agency, coined the term for Nike inspired by Gary Gilmore's last words. Gary Gilmore was an American criminal sentenced to death and when asked if he had any last words before being executed he simply said "Let's do it"

Tying that back to real estate, this is one of the biggest hurdles I have seen in new agents and, at times, some seasoned agents. Often people, especially perfectionists, want to ensure everything is exactly the way it "should be" before they take action. I've had new agents say, "Once I get my headshots and business cards, then I'll start prospecting." "Once I attend all these classes and trainings, then I will start letting people know I am a real estate agent." While, it's always good to have those things done, what's most important is to start NOW by taking action and building your business, hence the title of this section "Just do it!"

So for now, if someone asks for your contact information and you don't have a business card, just say "I just gave out my last card, can I get yours and I will promise to follow-up with you later today" In terms of doing all the training before you begin, there will always be more to learn and, while formal training and classes are vital, the best education is actually doing and hitting the pavement, literally. Start knocking on doors and start driving those streets to learn about neighborhoods and inventory. As the famous maxim goes, "Progress not perfection"

For a while, I was afraid to venture into the marketing world of videos. So many questions of how long it should be, what should I say, should I do it on my iPhone or hire a videographer, what if I look silly, etc. Finally I just went for it and it's been a great experience and I've learned a ton (more on that later).. I'm so happy I took that first step and you will be too.

By the way, if you have any interest in checking out my YouTube channel go to youtube.com/c/PaulFontaineRealtor. Lots of informative videos and definitely still a progress not perfection theme!

CHALLENGE: When you go to YouTube.com to check out my channel, take the first step and create your own channel. You will first need a gmail email account (go to gmail.com). Once you have a gmail address, you can then go to that account and click on YouTube and create an account. That is the first step to having your own YouTube Channel!

Be consistent

One of the most significant strategies in this book is being consistent and creating successful habits. As Stephen Covey once said "Our character is basically a composite of our habits. Because they are consistent, often unconscious patterns, they constantly, daily, express our character." Doing anything in this book once will yield you nothing or very little. Studies have shown that you have to send direct mail to a prospect up to 9 times before they recognize your name and/or brand. 9 times!! Calling one FSBO (For sale by Owner) and not securing an appointment is pretty typical. If you call 20 FSBOs, your success ratio will increase dramatically.

Success is hastened or delayed by one's habits. It is not one's passing inspirations or brilliant ideas so much as your everyday mental habits that control your life.
– Paramahansa Yogananda

Many new, or newer agents, have said to me "I'm going to see how it goes for the next few months and if it doesn't work out, I'll need to get a full time job" If that's your mindset, you've pretty much already solidified your fate as one of the 87% of agents no longer in the business. To be the exception, your business cannot be a hobby. If you want a business (and we'll discuss that next), you need to study those that are successful and have a productive daily schedule.

It tends to be human nature to be consistently inconsistent!

Some methods of staying focused and consistent are:

- Surrounding yourself with like minded agents

- Finding what parts of the business you are good at and bring you joy. It's only natural to continue doing things you enjoy.

- Having structure helps create habits to be consistent and also builds trust with clients, friends and family.

- Creating goals. It's challenging to stay focused if you don't know what you need to do. We will discuss more on this later in the book.

- Reward yourself. Even small rewards work. Like chocolate? Why not treat yourself to some dark chocolate after completing a project.

CHALLENGE: Ask yourself if you are being consistent with the most important aspects of my business?" Take a step back from yourself for a moment and act as if you were reviewing someone else's day to day activities. Do you see a consistent pattern each day regarding key elements of sustaining a successful business?

Understand you are building a business, not starting a new job.

Congratulations! You are a business owner. I always tell agents to run it like a business. Do you think a new business owner who just opened up their retail corner store would be successful if she only worked 4 days a week? How about if he only worked in the evenings because he had another job? It's highly probable they wouldn't be very successful. If you've ever opened up a store, or known someone who has, you'd know it is a very hard gig and business owners have to work long hours, especially for the first couple years, just to stay afloat. The most successful business owners work a lot more than 40 hours a week, sometimes 60-80 hrs. especially in the beginning.

Working in the real estate industry has so many amazing aspects to it including flexibility and an abundance of independence. Unlike a "normal" 9-5 job, independent contractors don't have a boss watching over us or co-workers wondering where we are if we are late to arrive for our shift. Many agents don't even come into the actual "brick and mortar" office anymore. This freedom can be challenging at times and we, as agents, need the discipline and accountability to work hard without anyone directly telling us to do it (your Why will help with that).

When building a business, track your expenses and sales and understand how much profit you are making. Successful business owners have long-term views of things and don't get bogged down on short periods of time where sales are down. I've worked with agents who sell millions in real estate, or have their teams that do, and at the end of the day, they aren't really sure how much money was left over for actual profit. Selling $25 million in real estate annually is amazing but if your expenses are too high you are wasting a lot of your time and money.

Deciding to commit yourself to long-term results rather than short-term fixes is as important as any decision you'll make in your lifetime.
-Tony Robbins

Work daily on your mindset

What you do daily becomes your habit and your habits create most of who you are in life. Keeping a positive mindset daily will help you deal with the roller coaster called real estate. There are a few things you can do to help achieve this task.

Another way to keep a positive mindset is to listen to motivational tapes, recordings, podcasts, etc. I have a lot of motivational speeches I got off iTunes a while ago and I listen to them often. It's amazing how differently you can feel after listening to someone cheering you on and motivating you.

It has been said that negative thinking can be more powerful than positive thinking and because of this, we need to be vigilant with this strategy. Negative thoughts can often "snowball" into an avalanche, so stopping your negative thought pattern a.s.a.p. is imperative. Sometimes literally just saying aloud "STOP!" can break the stream of thinking, even just for a moment, and help you steer the ship back towards a healthier mindset.

Cultivating your mind to yield positive thoughts is an important part of having the right mindset. Downplaying or detaching from the ever present negative thoughts is also essential. When you find yourself overwhelmed by negative thinking, one method of managing is to give that negative thinking a name. You can call it a person's name like George or even just a fictional name like "the jerk." It may seem a bit silly but giving your negative thoughts a separate name or identity helps you detach from them so you don't interpret those thoughts as who you are as a person.

Keep your thoughts positive because your thoughts become your words. Keep your words positive because your words become your behavior. Keep your behavior positive because your behavior becomes your habits. Keep your habits positive because your habits become your values. Keep your values positive because your values become your destiny.
– Mahatma Gandhi

In addition, visualizing success is a vital component to a professional athlete's performance and should be part of any agent's weekly routine. Some crucial aspects of visualizing are to create the picture or video in your mind as clearly, vividly and detailed as it can be. Making sure you are attaching a strong emotion to that picture or video is also integral. Lastly, having a strong belief that you can achieve, and are living that visualization is essential in helping to create a lasting impression on your psyche.

CHALLENGE: Write down 5-10 affirmations and read them aloud each morning and/or evening. Make sure you read them aloud. There's something about saying them and hearing the words that are more powerful than reading silently. While you are at it, tape those affirmations in your office or next to your bathroom mirror to see them numerous times a day.

Do whatever it takes: No excuses*.

*I put an asterisk next to this section because whatever you do, first and foremost, has to be legal by law and ethical per our industry's Code of Ethics. Beyond that, do whatever it takes to achieve success. There's a sign in my office that says "You can have reasons or results, you can't have both" This is one of the many BOLD laws taught at Keller Williams Realty.

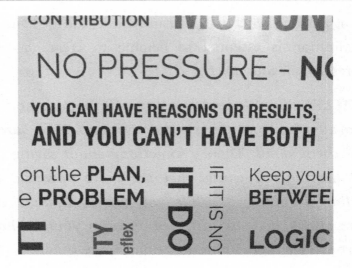

DON'T GIVE UP! If you have that mindset, then nothing is going to stop you. If you truly believe that you have to succeed NO MATTER WHAT, then I am sure that you will be the exception. It is when excuses start popping in your head, and you begin to hesitate, that success starts slipping through your fingers. If that happens, break your thought pattern and say, "I will succeed NO MATTER WHAT!" The phrase "no matter what" eliminates any excuses or options to not do it.

As days go on, there will be many times when things won't work out. If something doesn't work out, then you fix it. When the next thing doesn't work out, fix it again. Just recently I heard a newer agent Michael say "I'll give it 6 months and see how it goes, if it doesn't work out I'll have to get a regular job" I wasn't surprised at all to hear that Michael had abandoned the opportunity to be the exception by month #5. You are already setting yourself up for failure by giving yourself an out. The people that succeed are the people that fail the most. Don't be afraid to fail. The key to failing effectively is to learn from it and pivot to adjust your thinking, actions, processes, and systems.

It always seems impossible until it's done
-Nelson Mandela

Another sign in my office states "You can't deposit excuses" I always get a kick out of reading it as I sit at my desk. I know being an agent can be hard sometimes. I know it can be frustrating, especially if you are new to the business, but watch yourself when you begin to complain and immediately correct your mindset. Go back to your purpose and remind yourself of all the amazing things you'll experience and feel when you are successful. And while you're at it, think of all the pain and displeasure you will have if you fail. Both can be very motivating.

CHALLENGE: Search for motivational songs, speeches, podcasts or albums and download a few of your favorites.

Be thankful for what you have; you'll end up having more. If you concentrate on what you don't have, you will never, ever have enough.
—Oprah Winfrey

Be grateful

Every time I had a team meeting, I would go around the table and have each person discuss one thing they are grateful for today. To live a happy life, being grateful is essential and specifically being grateful with your real estate business is also critical to longevity. One simple strategy is to change the words "have to" into "get to" Instead of saying "I HAVE TO make calls for 2 hours today" you say "I GET TO make calls for 2 hours today" Do you see how that simple change affects your mindset and changes the statement from a bit negative to a more positive and grateful tone?

In the psychology world, this is called "reframing." Instead of dreading or complaining about certain aspects of our business, reframe it and be grateful to have the available time to make those calls (some people don't). Be thankful that you have a phone and an office to make those calls or thankful you have clients or a close group of friends, family and neighbors that you can call to offer your services. Be grateful you have the freedom and opportunities to grow your business and make as much money as you'd like.

In addition to being grateful for the things you have and get to do, be thankful for others. The magical words "thank you" go a long way in every aspect of life. Make it a mission to say thank you at least 10 times a day. It's really not that hard. You can thank someone for holding a door or an elevator, thank the cashier at your supermarket, thank the barista for your coffee, thank one of your employees for doing a good job, thank your client for choosing you out of all the agents in your area. The list goes on and on. While we are at it, I want to thank you for reading my book and for choosing to better yourself.

CHALLENGE: Keep a journal and each morning or evening write down 3 things you are grateful for that day. Periodically go back and read through past journal entries to remind yourself of the many blessings you have been given.

Hold yourself accountable

Keeping yourself accountable for your goals and your mission is a vital piece of the puzzle to be the exception. Some of the concepts discussed in this book will help hold yourself accountable such as writing down your goals and finding out your WHY.

When you create your goals, print them out and post them on

your bathroom mirror or on your office wall(next to your affirmations!). Better yet do both. If you feel you will have support from friends or family, send them your goals or post them on social media for your close friends and family to see. Nothing keeps you accountable and motivated then telling the whole world your goals!

Responsibility equals accountability equals ownership. And a sense of ownership is the most powerful weapon a team or organization can have.
– Pat Summitt

Numerous years ago I hired a business coach and he held me accountable on a weekly basis. Each week I had to fill out the same form detailing how many calls, appts, contracts and closings I had and compare those statistics to my set goals for that year. Coaches can help certain agents immensely but they can be pricey at times. If you can't afford a coach, ask your broker, team leader or just a fellow agent in the office to help you stay accountable. Every week for the past 3 years I have had an amazing and uplifting phone call with my friend, and fellow agent, Tracey where we either role-play or brainstorm or just share our highs and lows of the week.

CHALLENGE: Find an accountability buddy and make them a promise that you will call or text them once a day or week (whatever you choose) to give an update on your goals and initiatives.

Everyone is a potential client or referral. ACT THAT WAY..

A fellow agent I know always used to say "I'm a public figure." I always rolled my eyes a bit, but it's actually true. We, as real estate agents, are public figures. Not in the traditional sense of the phrase as it pertains to politicians or celebrities, but we are out there in the public's eye. Our faces are on signs, billboards, bus stop benches, supermarket shopping carts (carriages as we used to call them in New England). Our names are on for sale signs throughout towns and cities. Some of our advertisements are still in newspapers and magazines. Google us and, if you are doing a good job marketing, your name will come up all over the first page of search results. We are public figures. Our job is to be known.

I've seen, and heard of, real estate agents being kicked out of professional sporting events for rude or drunken behavior. I know of agents who have done unlawful or unethical things in their businesses. I've seen many social media posts that in my opinion do not shine the best light on that particular agent.

We are being hired to help, guide and advise buyers and sellers in probably their biggest financial decision of their lives. Nobody wants some unruly guy getting escorted out of a football game as his or her representative. It can be challenging at times as you may feel like you are never free to "let your hair down" but this is part of owning a business and part of being a respected and trusted advisor for clients.

Everyone is a potential client or referral. TREAT THEM THAT WAY.

No, you aren't having déjà vu. It's similar to the last section's title but the ending is different.   Everyone you come in contact with may want to buy, sell, rent or invest in real estate, now or in the future or may know someone who does. Treat them that way.   It's easy to go about your day and not think about this fact.

How many times do you go to the dry cleaners and talk to the owners or get coffee and chat with the same barista. I've even gotten sales from past dates that didn't work out! You never know who may be looking to do a real estate transaction. Treat everyone like they are your next client.

What exactly does that mean? It doesn't mean continually badgering everyone asking if they want to sell their house. It doesn't mean act like you are interested in their life because you hope to make some money off them eventually. Treating everyone like a potential client means keeping in touch, asking about their life and continually adding value to their life. We will discuss this in detail later in the book. If you keep this mindset, you will reap the rewards of a long and successful business and you will, no doubt, <u>be the exception</u>!

SECTION 2

SUCCESSFUL AGENT TIPS AND STRATEGIES

To be successful in real estate, you must always and consistently put your clients' best interests first. When you do, your personal needs will be realized beyond your greatest expectations. -Anthony Hitt

SET GOALS!!!!!!

This section could be its own book as it is one of the most important requirements for becoming a successful agent (and a successful and happy person in my opinion).

Long ago I learned the ACRONYM **SMART: Specific, Measurable, Attainable, Realistic and Timely.** I, in general, subscribe to this thinking though I think the "A" and "R" can be up for some debate. Your goals need to be specific because if they are a vague statement such as " sell a lot of real estate" how will you ever know if you achieve it? Is that $1 million in sales? $5 million? $50 million? If you aren't **Specific** you will never know what you are striving for, how much more you have to go to attain, etc.

Measurable is the next one. Obviously you need to be able to assess how you are doing with a goal, so having measurable goals is needed. Setting a goal to Sell $1 million/month is measurable because at the end of the month you can add up your sales and see if it gets to $1 million.

Attainable and **Realistic** are the two that some may have questions about. Some experts will say "Reach for the moon and even if you fail, you can still hit a star." These items are subjective and you can decide what realistic and attainable mean to you. My recommendation is to always push yourself just one step further than you are comfortable. If you think $2 million in sales is a realistic and attainable goal, set it at $2.2 or $2.4 million. I have often found when you stretch your goals, you stretch your brain. Setting your sights a little higher forces you to think more outside the box and creatively find ways to achieve results never before achieved.

Lastly, **Timely** is key. You can have a specific, measurable and realistic goal, but if you don't put a due date it's not overly useful. Setting a time limit is essential. Do you want to achieve that goal in a month or a year? How about setting goals for the day? It's all up to you, but giving yourself that due date helps you focus and motivate yourself.

So, time to take a break from reading and learning. It's time to implement one of our first lessons of "Just Do It." Do you have goals you have written down for this year? If so, congratulations.

According to the best research, less than 3 percent of Americans have written goals.
-Brian Tracy

If you haven't written down your goals, let's work on that now. To keep it simple, let's do 3 business goals and 3 personal goals. Remember the acronym SMART and make sure they are specific, measurable, attainable, realistic and timely.

CHALLENGE: *If you have not set and written down your goals, take a day or two this week and work on it. To keep it simple, decide on your goal for:*

- *Number of appointments per year (divide by 52 to get a weekly goal)*

- *Number of signed buyer and seller client contracts per year*

- *Number of settlements (broken out between # of buyers and sellers)*

- *Estimate average sales price of each settlement*

- *Total sales dollar volume goal for the year (ave sales price * number of settlements)*

Prioritize Daily

Life as an agent can be chaotic. I typically receive over 100 emails each day. Add on phone calls from leads, clients, realtors and salespeople. While we are at it, numerous text exchanges throughout the day. It's easy to feel frazzled. I have a simple habit each day of writing down the top 5 things I want to achieve each day, prioritize them from #1-#5 then and start working immediately on #1. Once #1 is done, I start work on #2 and so on. This helps keep you focused in a world where it's easy, even for the most self disciplined, to lose track of what's most important. Some people prefer to write the list the night before so they are ready as soon as they start their day. Others prefer to do it first thing in the morning and use that momentum to kickoff the day.

How do you prioritize, you ask? There are different methods and some effective ones are ranking tasks that are due the soonest or prioritizing projects that will be the most beneficial to your business. If you ask any real estate expert, one of those top 5 prioritized tasks should always be lead generation. That item should be on your list every day of every week. So you're welcome, I've already given you one of the answers, now you have to figure out the four other priorities each day!

CHALLENGE: Write down you top 5 things you'd like to accomplish today, then prioritize them and get started on

#1.

Time Block Your Schedule

This is another very simple strategy that will help you <u>be the exception</u> once implemented. After you prioritize tasks for your day, the next step is to put those priorities into your schedule. Each item needs to be put into a specific time slot on your calendar. Once that is complete, you DO IT! The crucial part of time blocking is to not be distracted by anything else except what is on your calendar for that time period. If you scheduled lead generation from 10am-12pm and it's 10:15am, you shouldn't be doing anything else but lead generation. Not checking emails, not responding quickly to that text. Nothing but lead generation.

If you go through the effort of prioritizing your day and scheduling those tasks but don't do them, then you have just wasted a lot of your precious time. A study in the <u>Journal of Experimental Psychology: Human Perception and Performance</u> (Vol. 27, No. 4) states that multitasking is less efficient because it takes extra time to shift mental gears every time you switch between tasks. Stick to the task you have deemed as your priority and follow your schedule.

Remember: 1. Prioritize. 2. Schedule in specific time blocks. 3. DO IT!

Write Handwritten Notes

When you pick up your mail and there are a bunch of envelopes and one of them is handwritten, which envelope do you open first?   Of course, it would be the handwritten one! Everyone likes to feel special and a handwritten note sends a message to people that they matter and that you took time out of your busy schedule to write to them. I recommend writing notes for lots of different opportunities. Some ideas are:

1. Thank open house attendees

2. Thank owners after meeting with them on a listing appt.

3. Congratulations to clients after settlements.

4. Birthday and anniversary cards(either wedding or home purchase anniversaries)

5. Thank you for your referral

Buy some nice note cards with either your initials on the front or have your real estate agency logo on them. Sometimes you can even get away with some cute or funny ones depending on your clientele and relationships. Last year I sent my clients 3D valentine's day cards for kids. Everyone loves to laugh or smile.

One of the things we previously discussed is GRATITUDE.

Writing a note to someone to express your gratitude is a wonderful way of killing two birds with one stone. Some ideas of who to write notes to include past or current clients, other agents, vendors, mortgage, title and insurance contacts, your sphere, etc. Remember everyone is a potential client or referral ;)

CHALLENGE: Write out one hand-written note today. It can be to anyone. Don't overthink it, just sit down and begin. A few days later when you get a call or text from that person saying how sweet it was to get your card, you'll be glad you did it!

Make Appointments to See Inventory

We are hired and contracted with buyers, sellers and renters to be experts. It is our duty to know what is for sale in your market. Obviously, we can't see all the homes for sale at one time (at least not in big cities), but you can certainly see a broad range of places so you have a general idea of what a $200,000 house looks like vs. a $500,000 house.

It's important to know your inventory. You should be seeing as many properties as possible. If you are new and don't have any clients, schedule preview appointments to see places for sale and start educating yourself on what is available and what buyers get for certain price points. As we will discuss later in the book, you should always be creating and adding value for your clients. Making appointments to see properties and being on top of your market's inventory is one of the best ways of doing this.

CHALLENGE: *Schedule 5 appointments this week to view some homes you haven't seen in an area you want to specialize in or a new area you aren't familiar with yet.*

Be in the Office. Get to Know other Agents.

When I first started I was in the office often and as I got to know other agents and they saw my hard work ethic, they began to give me leads they didn't want or couldn't handle. From my experience, leads that seasoned agents with 10-20 years under their belt don't want are often leads a new agent is more than happy to take! Even rental leads are a good way to start your business. Often other agents don't want to handle those and are happy to have a hard working new agent take them with no referral fees paid.

Call me old fashioned. I know the trend is that many agents, and workers in general, are not coming into traditional offices as often as before. I still think it's important to be in the office everyday. Even if it's just for an hour or so.

Real estate is a relationship business, both with clients and with other real estate agents. I have too many examples to list here where I have reaped the rewards of being in the office. Working "floor time" and taking "sign calls" can also be helpful and that traditionally entails being in the office.

Sometimes you get leads that walk in the door and who do you think has the best chance of capturing those leads? You or someone who just works from their home? How many leads are walking into your home? Exactly, zero.

My friend, and fellow agent, Tracey likes to go into the office each day but, she always makes sure she makes her lead generation calls first so she's not distracted. She makes those calls from home where she can focus and then goes into the office afterwards. Every agent is different so it is up to you to decide where and when is best for your activities.

Find a Niche and be a "King or Queen!"

"There's riches in the niches" is something I once heard. If you have ever taken a marketing course, you know the term "niche" or "niche market" . The concept is simple. Rather than spending your time trying to become an expert on every neighborhood or attempting to be the "go to agent" for every buyer, seller, investor, or renter in your state, you can decide on a specific area or type of client to focus on. Some agents specialize in luxury buyers, while others decide they are most comfortable with first time homebuyers. Maybe someone in your family is in the service and you want to specialize in helping veterans with VA loans. The niche is up to you.

Other niches can be the type of real estate deals. Do you want to focus on new construction or maybe work with professional flippers who buy, renovate, and sell? In the classes I teach in my office, I recommend my students be the "king or queen" of just their block or development. Here's how you become the "king or queen." If you just focus on 50-100 neighbors and on average owners move every 8-10 years that's a potential of around 7-8 listings per year. Be the agent that those neighbors think of first when they decide to list their home. Being the first agent neighbors think of is extremely important. Studies by the National Association of REALTORS show that over 75% of homeowners only contacted one agent before finding the right one to sell their home.

Lastly, look for a void and fill that gap. Maybe the market has turned a bit soft and there are now more foreclosures or short sales you could focus on. A way to find a void is by analyzing the turnover rate. There's a simple way of finding out the turnover rate of a neighborhood to understand how often owners sell in that area.

Take the total # of homes SOLD (in the area you want to analyze) and divide by total # of homes (in that same area) = real estate turnover rate (for that specific area).

For example, if I want to focus my marketing on the development where I live and it's a large community of 150 homes, I take that 150, which is total # of homes (in the development). I then go to my local MLS and pull all homes in that development that sold this past year. Let's say that's 13.

We take 13 sold that year/ 150 total homes = 8.7% turnover rate (for my development).

So, in an average year, 11.5% of homes sell. This % is important but doesn't mean much unless you are able to compare it to other neighborhoods or areas. At this time we don't know if 11.5% is high, low or average without analyzing other areas.

As agents, we want to focus on neighborhoods or communities with the highest historical turnover because that means there's a higher probability of owners deciding to sell each year.

If we use an average sales price of $250,000 and 2.75% commission for the example above, that's close to $7K gross commission * 13 listings = $91,000 gross commission per year! Would you like to make that? Earning that much per year would put you in approximately the top 15% of agents in the country! That's how to <u>be the exception</u>!

CHALLENGE: I recommend doing this simple analysis for numerous other neighborhoods and communities to get 5-10 different data points for you to see if there is a void you can fill and become the real estate "king or queen" for that high turnover area.

Read Daily

I love to read and it has been very helpful in my career with running a business. As always, you can't just read things and think everything will magically happen. You have to implement the ideas and strategies you have absorbed from the readings.

One of my favorite business books is Gary Keller's <u>The Millionaire Real Estate Agent.</u> I have one copy on my bedroom nightstand and one in my drawer in my office. I look through it quite often. It's a guidebook and a book of answers. Remember back in elementary school where they had answers in the back of the textbook or, even better, you find the teacher's version of the textbook with all the answers. That's how I describe Gary's book.

Some of my other favorites are:

- Start with Why and Find your Why - Simon Sinek

- Don't sweat the small stuff - Richard Carlson

- Go for No! - Andrea Waltz and Richard Fenton

- A Better Way to Live - Og Mandino

- The Miracle Morning - Hal Elrod

- Profit First - Mike Michalowicz

- The Compound Effect - Darren Hardy

- The Positive Thinking Secret - Aaron Kennard

- Awaken the Giant Within - Anthony Robbins

- Fred Factor - Mark Sanborn

- The Millionaire Real Estate Agent - Gary Keller

- Designing Your Life - Bill Burnett and Dave Evans

CHALLENGE: Choose one of the books listed, purchase it and read chapter each day.

Learn! Go to Seminars, Webinars and Conferences.

I am a big fan of learning and training and this is one of main reasons I moved my business to Keller Williams Realty. Going to trainings, watching a webinar, attending conferences are all great ways to learn and grow as a professional. You gain expert knowledge and have opportunities to network with other potential referral agents. Want the best way to learn? Teach! The more I teach, the more I continue to have to push myself to learn more and become an expert.

The best leaders are the best learners.
-Harvard Business Review

CHALLENGE: Research upcoming seminars, conferences or webinars in your company and sign up for one this week.

Learn, but More Importantly Implement.

The previous section about learning is very relevant but it's useless at the same time, unless you implement what you've learned. I remember this young agent that seemed to have so much potential. For months, I would see her at all of the training sessions taking notes. Then, as time went on, I noticed her absence on a regular basis. After a period of time, I finally asked the broker if she'd see Wendy lately. My broker said she had left the office a few weeks ago stating she couldn't make it in the business.

How many times have you come out of a class or conference full of notes and to do's, only to get caught up in the daily grind and never implement any of those items? Don't worry, it's happened to all of us. My recommendation is to go through all your notes and put a star next to 2-3 items you'd like to prioritize. Start with #1 and take a step toward implementing that item. Once that's done, take another step. It doesn't matter if it's large or small as long as you are progressing toward that goal. I often type in goals or priorities into my phone calendar with an alert that pops up everyday reminding me of what to focus on.

Don't be a Secret Agent.

This is one of my favorite sayings in the real estate world. Our job is to get our name out there and make people think of us first when they need any real estate assistance. Don't be a secret agent!   If you've been in this business for at least a couple of years, you've probably experienced that frustrating moment when you bump into a friend or see a post on Facebook from an acquaintance excited to announce they just purchased a new home!   It's never a good feeling in your gut. You are happy for your friend and frustrated with yourself for being a secret agent.   Sometimes agents get mad at their friends and say, "Why didn't you call me?"   I'm sorry to tell you it's not their fault, it's yours.   This is your business.   It's not their obligation to remember you are an agent.

CHALLENGE: Tell at least 1 new person each day that you are in real estate and ask them how you can help.

Be an Amazing Agent

Most successful agents who have been in the business for 5-10+ years get most of their business from previous clients and referrals from them. It starts on day 1 of your business. Act professionally and don't talk badly about other agents or your clients. Give your clients more than they expect. Go that extra step to stand out among the thousands of agents. If you are an amazing agent, most of these strategies in this book will fall into place.

I often say half of your job is being a therapist. People often buy or sell because major life situations are going on in their lives.   As someone once coined the phrase "the 3 Ds". Death, Divorce and Diapers.   Three of the biggest reasons for buying or selling real estate. Someone dies, you need to sell your house. New baby is born, you need a bigger house. Husband just got a promotion and transferred to another state, you need to sell. Partner just got fired and you can't afford your home anymore, you need to sell.

Our job is to be there for our clients in their time of need. Our job is to guide them through this, often, complex process. It is an amazing privilege to have that opportunity and I cherish it each day. This is what being an amazing agent is all about and how to be the exception.

Be Aggressive.

Not many clients want someone weak negotiating on their behalf. The word aggressive can sometimes have a negative connotation, but it doesn't have to in this circumstance. Being aggressive means you treat the deal like it's your own. It means you will stay on top of the other agent to make sure things are done on time. Being aggressive means following up consistently with leads. Being aggressive is asking more and more questions and digging more deeply to get to the real reasons and motivations of your clients. Being aggressive is fighting for every dollar for your client.

Some people thought I should use the word "assertive" for this section of the book instead of aggressive. While I can understand where they are coming from, I stand by the word aggressive. Any word that creates an emotional reaction is the type of behavior that can propel you to beat the odds and that's what this book is all about. **Invest in Real Estate**

I've always been an advocate for owning your own home and also investing in real estate. As someone whose business is to help people buy homes and educate them why it's a smart decision to own their own home, it seems counterintuitive to not want the same for yourself. How can you convince someone else it's such a smart thing to do if you haven't done it yourself? Plus, as an agent, there are so many benefits to buying real estate. 95% of the time you make a commission when you buy properties! That's amazing. You get back 2-3% off of the sales price automatically. And that's even before you begin negotiating the price. It's fantastic.

Don't wait to buy real estate. Buy real estate and wait.
-Will Rogers

There are so many benefits to owning property and using the leverage of low down payment mortgages for your own home is a great way to begin. Other investing options include: flipping properties, wholesaling or renting out investment properties. I can write a whole other book about the benefits of investing in real estate. It is one of the best methods to accumulate long term wealth.

CHALLENGE: Make a formal, written goal to purchase a property within the next year. Either a primary residence or an investment property.

If you're a brand new agent, have 3-4 months of expenses saved.

You passed your real estate exam and now you are officially a real estate agent. Congrats! Unlike a traditional corporate job, you aren't getting a weekly paycheck on a guaranteed, consistent basis. You don't want to go through all the work of becoming an agent to be forced to quit after 2-3 months because you have no savings to pay your rent or car loan. It is vital to have a minimum 3-4 months of savings to pay for all of your usual expenses. Some would say 5-6 months worth of savings. Even if you miraculously sell a house the first week you begin, it still takes usually 45-60 days to settle on that property so you are already at almost 2 months of no income even in the most optimistic situation.

CHALLENGE: Do you know what your expenses are each month? If not, go through bills, receipts and bank statements and create a spreadsheet of all your expenses for the past month. I use Reprophet.com to track all of my expenses.

Develop a budget and P&L

I know, I know. Sounds boring and let's be serious, who likes to develop budgets? Sometimes it's the most mundane and painful things that reap the most rewards. As an agent, you will be bombarded by sales people trying to sell you on their services whether it's helping generate Facebook leads, sending you online leads a company generates or mailing out magazines with your face on them. You need to understand where your money goes and how much income comes in so creating a P&L statement (Profit & Loss) is important.

A budget is more related to your personal life and I'd recommend starting with putting together a simple budget of what is the total cost you need to "survive" including rent, utilities, loans, food, etc. to get your total monthly expenses. Once you know what your total expenses are you can then begin to decide how much on top of that you'd like to save and have to spend on non essential things like vacations. This will also help when you begin to develop your business P&L as you need to set goals in your estimated P&L for the year that is consistent with your budget numbers. If your budget numbers are higher than your budgeted income in your business P&L then you have a problem.

In general, a P&L looks like this:

GCl $ (Gross Commission Income Earned)

- Cost of Goods Sold (Pertains more if you are a team leader and have Fees paid for splits with agents on team. Does include referral fees to outside agents though)

- Operating Expenses (costs paid for admin support, marketing, dues, insurance, fees, etc)

Net Profit $

Profit Margin % (Net PRofit $ / GCI $)

Most experts say the goal is to have a profit margin % between 30+%.

If you'd like my personal budget for my business feel free to send me an email: Paul@BestPhillyHomes.com

Qualify your leads

We've all been there. You get a call and are super excited that someone wants to speak to you about real estate and you think back to whatever training you may have had and say to yourself "set the appt!" You make the appt to show a property, meet them at the home and find out the buyer isn't financially ready to purchase whether because of debts or personal situations, etc.   It's happened to all of us at some point.

Make sure you ask questions before you spend too much time with a lead (I wouldn't even call them clients yet).

Buyer lead qualifying questions:

1. Are you purchasing with cash or getting a mortgage?

2. Are you pre approved for a mortgage?

3. Are you working with a real estate agent?

4. When are you looking to move?

5. What areas or neighborhoods are they interested in?

6. Why are they looking to buy?

7. What price range do they want to stay within?

8. How many bedrooms and bathrooms do they require?

9. Do you need to sell your home in order to purchase the next one?

Seller lead qualifying questions:

1. Why are you looking to move?

2. Do you have to sell your home in order to purchase the next one?

3. What is your outstanding loan balance?

4. When are you looking to move?

5. What is most important to you in this sale?

6. What are you looking for in your next agent?

7. Are you interviewing other agents?

8. Do you have a listing price in mind?

All of those questions and more will help you guide them in

the right direction and also save yourself time.

Create value

One of our biggest requirements to being a successful real estate agent is to continually add value to the people with whom we come into contact. Whether it's communicating to our database, showing a buyer a home or sitting at a seller's kitchen table discussing the sale of their home, you must focus on adding value to that person. We are hired to be experts.

Often people ask "How much is my home worth?" or "How's the market doing?" Knowing that these are probably the top two questions we are asked, make it your goal to keep everyone you know, and all your present and past clients, informed with recent, relevant information and stats answering these questions.

Some of my long-time clients call me often to ask about their taxes and if their assessments are accurate. Others call and ask me if it's worth putting in a new kitchen and how much will it add to the value of their home. These are all questions we, as agents, can help with and it's a way to add value. Have the mindset that everyone can benefit from "having" an agent, not just when they are buying or selling real estate.

CHALLENGE: Brainstorm and write down 3-5 value add items you could give to leads or clients. Some examples are market updates, refinance information, home selling tips, contractor recommendation lists, etc.

Help your clients achieve their goals.

If you help your clients achieve their goals, you will be in business for a long time. Period. Some agents state their sales goals, not in terms of how many millions of dollars they will sell in real estate but, in how many families they want to help each year. For example, "This year my goal is to help 26 families achieve their real estate dreams." It's your job to find out what your clients' goals are and then help them achieve those goals. One way of doing this is highlighted in the next section.

Ask questions and dig deep with leads/clients

Nothing will help you better understand your clients' needs than asking them questions. Sometimes in this fast paced world, we assume to know what a client is looking for or we ask a question or two and assume we have a handle on things. It isn't until you ask the 3rd or 4th or even 7th follow-up question that you get to the core of their wants and needs.

Here's a possible dialogue-

You: "What is your goal?"

Client: "To buy a house"

You : "Do you want a condo or a rowhome?"

Client: "A condo I think"

You: "Great, do you have a preference for a high rise or low/mid rise or small boutique condo building?"

Client: "I'm not sure, probably boutique"

You "Okay, is having a front desk or 24 hr. security staff important to you?

Client: 'Yes"

You: "Ok, most boutique buildings do not offer this, usually you would have to be in mid to high rise condo building. What is most important to you, having 24 hr security staff or living in a boutique building?"

The conversation can continue and as you can see by asking more and more specific questions, you start to get a better understanding of their desires. Digging deep gets you to the core of people's motivations and also clears up any assumptions or grey areas that exist.

Ask questions and dig deep with other agents

I can always tell which brand new agents will <u>be the exception</u> or at least which ones have the highest probability of lasting longer than most. I can tell because **they are not afraid to ask questions**. If I'm teaching a class in my office and I ask if anyone has questions, the exceptional agent will raise their hand. Agents who ask questions, and are eager to learn, have a much higher chance of succeeding. I'm always astonished when I finish teaching a class with a group of new agents and there are no questions or few questions. After over 17 years in real estate, I still attend classes and ask questions. We will never know everything and you will always need to learn more. Don't be afraid to ask questions. It doesn't make you look stupid, it makes you look smart.

Don't be afraid to say, "I don't know"

Continuing in the same vein from the previous section, when a client asks you a question and you don't know, or aren't sure, don't be afraid to say "I don't know, I will find out and get back to you a.s.a.p." It's okay. While it's always a good feeling when you can answer a question, many new agents are scared into inaction sometimes because they ask, "What if I don't know the answer?" It's okay. Buyers and sellers have a lot of questions and you will never know all the answers. Just when I think I've heard it all, I get a new question I've never heard before from a client.

Having said all this, it is vital that you do in fact get back to the client asap. Too often I have experienced someone telling me they'll get right back to me with an answer and I never hear from them. It's okay to say "I don't know", it's not okay to promise someone an answer and not fulfill.

Follow-up, follow-up, follow-up

Not following up with your prospects is the same as filling up your bathtub without first putting the stopper in the drain.
-Michelle Moore

Generating leads is one of your top priorities, but if you only contact a lead once and let them fall by the wayside, you are making one of the biggest mistakes in real estate. Studies show you need, on average, 6 contact attempts before receiving a reply and up to 7 successful contacts with someone before they recognize your name or brand. Most sales tend to happen from follow-up, not from the initial contact. The majority of agents will stop after the first or second contact. Let me repeat that: MOST sales will come from your follow-up calls, emails, texts, etc. NOT from the initial contact.

Here are some interesting stats:

2% of Sales are made in the first contact

3% of Sales are made in the second contact

5% of Sales are made in the third contact

10% of Sales are made in the fourth contact

80% of sales are made in the fifth to twelfth contact

Only 12% of sales people make more than three contact attempts to a lead.

INFOGRAPHIC BY WWW.SULATA.NET

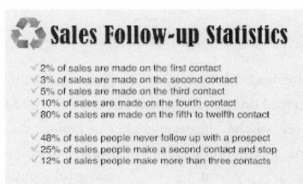

Reply quickly.

Everything is fast these days and if you aren't fast also, you may be in trouble. I've gotten a call, email or text from an online lead requesting information on a listing or asking to see a place and I've replied to them a couple hours after and they had already moved on and found another agent to help them. It's understandable that you can't be available 24 hours a day; it's just the state of the real estate industry.

Until you convince people otherwise, many believe agents are all the same, so they will just click another button while they are online searching for homes and find

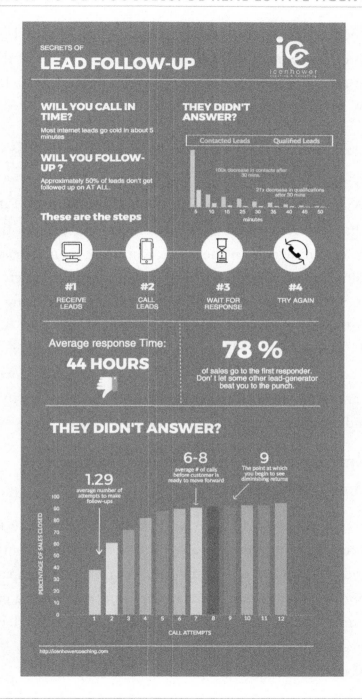

someone else to show them the house. Also as a tip, I have found if someone doesn't answer your call, try texting them right after you leave a voice message. Often people will not answer their phone but they will reply to a text.

Be Part of Office Leadership or Join Committees

At Keller Williams, there is something called the ALC, Associate Leadership Council.   When I worked at Berkshire Hathaway, there wasn't as formal of a committee, but there were certain agents in the office who were seen as leaders helping and supporting the broker with office events, etc.   I have sold houses to people I have met while volunteering and coordinating events for my office. Being part of your office and "giving back" will always help you in your business. Studies show that volunteering in the business world enhances teamwork, improves culture, and enhances your brand image in the eyes of our clients and customers

Think of a catchy nickname or tag line for people to remember.

After having worked closely with Mike McCann "The Real Estate Man" for over 13 years, I am honored to call him a friend..   Mike has repeatedly been awarded his company's honor of #1 real estate agent in the country.. He is a great example of this strategy.   Very rarely, if ever, do I hear someone say his name without saying the full moniker. "Mike McCann The Real Estate Man"

Around 10 years ago (after deciding nothing great rhymes with my last name Fontaine), I came up with the very simple "Call Paul" tagline and it stuck. People yell out "Call Paul" on the streets to me or post it online. My license plate has my tag line on it also. My advice is to think of something very simple and catchy and use it everywhere. Put your tagline on email signatures, website URLs, online ads, brochures, car wraps, whatever and wherever you can. The goal in marketing, especially brand marketing, is to have people remember you. The easier, and catchier it is, the more people see it and the faster you will build your business. With consistent brand marketing comes leads and name recognition. #CallPaul :)

Find a mentor

Why reinvent the wheel? As many success coaches, books and articles recommend, find someone who has already achieved the level of success that you want and spend time with them. Take them to lunch, ask them lots of questions. Ask them to be your mentor. If they say no, find someone else. Just like in sales, you may have to go through some "no's" to get to some "yes's")

Mentors have the experience you desire and can help speed up your progress by guiding you past some hurdles they have learned how to overcome. Mentors can encourage you, empathize with you, and give you unbiased opinions on things.

Long ago, I realized that success leaves clues, and that people who produce outstanding results do specific things to create those results. I believed that if I precisely duplicated the actions of others, I could reproduce the same quality of results that they had.
-Tony Robbins

CHALLENGE: Think about who you know that would be a good mentor. Who do you admire? Who have you learned from previously? Can't think of anyone? Then think about where you could go in order to find someone that could be helpful?   Local real estate organization?   Chamber of commerce? Your alma mater?

Know your numbers.

As the saying goes "measure what matters." Numbers scare a lot of people so they may shy away from this part of running a business. Don't be afraid. The numbers you need to know are not complicated but very crucial in knowing what you need to improve upon.   By knowing your numbers, it automatically creates a plan of action for you each day helping you more easily focus on your priorities.

Some pertinent figures you should track are:

a) Number of closings per year

b) Total Sales (Add up the sold price for each closing)

c) Average sales price per closing (Line B/Line A)

d) Gross Commission Income Earned-GCIE (Line C * average commission %*Line A)

e) Number of contacts that turned into actual qualified leads (%)

f) Number of qualified leads that turned into appointments (%)

g) Number of appointments that turned into signed contracts (%)

h) Number of signed contracts (listings and buyers) that turned into actual closings. (%)

For example, if you've been in the business for a year or more and you've tracked your numbers for your business your hypothetical results might look like this:

Sales Numbers to know:

a) Number of closings per year: 10

b) Total Sales: $2,500,000

c) Average sales price: $250,000 ($2,500,000/10)

d) GCIE: $75,000 ($250,000 * 3%(.03) * 10

Conversion Rate Numbers to know:

a) 240 contacts made to people that converted into finding 50 qualified leads looking to buy or sell (divide 50 leads by 240 contacts = 21% conversion)

b) 50 qualified leads converted to 25 actual appointments/meetings (divide 25 appointments by 50 leads = 50% conversion)

c) 25 buyer or seller appointments turned into 15 contracts signed (divide 15 contracts by 25 appointments = 60% conversion)

d) 15 buyer or listing contracts signed turned into 10 actual closings (divide 10 closings by 15 contracts = 67% conversion)

In summary:

Number of contacts made in past year: 240

Number of qualified leads from those contacts: 50

Number of actual appointments from those contacts: 25

Number of contracts signed from those appointments: 15

Number of contracts that turned into actual closings: 10

Once you have historic data, you can use the figures to set annual goals and build a business plan. Here's another great calculation. Want to set goals for next year? If you take the previous number of contacts made 240 and divide it by number of closings 10 we get 24. What the number 24 represents is how many people you need to contact in order to get 1 closing. Want to have 2 additional closings next year? Talk to 48 more people next year (24 * 2 closings). It's as simple as that.

If you are brand new and need to guesstimate, a simple way of establishing foundational figures is to set a GCIE goal then find out what the average sales price is for your area or for your office. With those figures you can calculate your number of closings goal.

Let;s say you decide $60,000 is your GCIE goal for your first year. After researching average sales price, either by speaking to your broker or pulling statistics from your MLS, you find out the average sales price in your area is $200,000. If we assume a 3% commission, just for this example, ($200,000 * .03) we get a commision of $6,000 per closing. If $60,000 is our goal and you make $6,000 per closing, we divide $60,000 by $6,000 and get 10 closings. Now you have a specific plan.

To dive even deeper into those numbers you can break out those 240 leads over a weekly time span and (assuming 2 weeks off a year) leaving you with 50 weeks you can divide the 240 leads by 50 weeks = 5 leads a week (approx). Now you have a specific and timely goal just as we discussed previously in this book. Each week it is your goal to get 5 leads.

Keep in mind, conversion rates can vary significantly. Some studies show that conversion rates for online leads like Facebook and Google ads are 1-5% or less. My assumptions for the above example were that at least half of your leads will be coming from your close network of family, friends, neighbors and also their friends. Those types of leads will convert at a much higher rate than an online lead typically.

The more experienced you are and the more you practice what to say and how to handle objections, the better your conversion rates will be.

Be likable and trustworthy.

People do business with agents they like and trust. It certainly also helps if you are knowledgeable and know what you are doing, but most importantly people need to like you and trust you in order to decide that you are the one they'd like to represent them. A big tip on how to increase the chances of someone liking you: **show appreciation.** Throughout this book, we discuss being grateful and showing appreciation. Utilize these concepts when conducting business and, quite honestly, anytime.

Another way to help people like you is to identify and understand their behavioral style. One popular method of doing this is through the behavioral assessment tool entitled DISC. There's a lot to know and learn about this process so I'll try to keep it relatively short and sweet for now. DISC is an acronym for Dominance, Influence, Steadiness and Conscientiousness. This system utilizes a series of questions and answers to place you into one or two categories so you can better understand yourself and others.

For example, if you are identified in the D category you are the type of person that is very direct, good at seeing things on a macro level and also probably a bit impatient. You don't want to be telling long stories to someone in the D category! On the other hand if someone is in the I category then they probably enjoy getting together and having lunch and chatting and would love to hear that long story. People tend to like people that they connect with and feel a common bond and doing your best to speak to them in a manner they prefer goes a long way toward helping build likeability and trust. Next time you are speaking with someone see if you can identify what style they prefer and see how things go when you can mirror their tonality, speed of talking and overall mannerisms.

CHALLENGE: Never taken the DISC personality test? Go to discpersonalitytesting.com to take a free DISC test.

Practice scripts and roleplay

Being a successful agent isn't all about showing pretty houses. We are salespeople and you have to accept that fact and embrace it. Our goal is to sell ourselves and to sell our listings. As a salesperson, much of our life will be speaking with clients and potential leads. A lot of agents hate the word "scripts." I may have been in that group at one point in my life. Professional athletes don't wait until the game to practice; they do it before they get on the field. So then why would you practice on your clients? Preparation is key and you must practice consistently how to respond to questions and objections. The more you practice, the more natural it will sound and the less you will stumble over your words.

Part of practicing scripts is to role-play, so finding a role-play partner and/or mentor is essential. When choosing someone, make sure you have someone you are comfortable with and someone who will be honest with you. Having someone who just says you are doing well with no effective criticism isn't going to help you grow and improve.

CHALLENGE: Choose a specific area of business you want to practice such as listing presentations, buyer presentations, objection handling or lead conversion. If you are a Keller Williams agent there are plenty of scripts available to study and practice. If your company doesn't offer that, I would recommend searching online for "realtor scripts" or check out tomferry.com or theclose.com.

SECTION 3

TOP 25 LEAD GENERATING TOOLS

You Are Out of Business If You Don't Have a Prospect
-Zig Zagler

This final section of the book will concentrate on specific tools for building your business. Generating leads is a vital aspect of owning a real estate business. For many of these, I had added the word "FREE" to emphasize how many options you have that don't cost any money (or very little). I always recommend starting with the free strategies first and then once you have sales under your belt you can entertain spending some money for other options.

I'd also like to emphasize that there is no one great lead generation tool that will solve every agent's quest for success. Every agent is different and each person has certain aspects of lead generation that they prefer over others. Just like finding an exercise regimen that you enjoy, you need to find which lead generation tools work best for you. Any one of these tools can help you become a successful agent as long as you do it consistently and continually improve.

Make a customer, not a sale.
-Katherine Barchetti

1. Contact FOR SALE BY OWNERS (FSBOs) and Expired Listings   FREE BUT COULD VARY

Getting listings is one of the top things every agent should be focused on and who better to communicate with than people who own homes and want to sell?   That's the definition of FSBOs and Expireds. They have raised their hand and said, "I want to sell my house" As with anything that is worthwhile, it can take a lot of work to convert these owners into clients but it's a great source of business for many successful agents.

If you want to call these homeowners, there are methods that are free or you can pay numerous companies to send you contact information for a monthly fee. When you drive by a FSBO sign on a house, stop, take a picture of the sign and knock on their doors. Being first always gives you a better chance of getting a listing appt. At the very least, you get to tour a house for sale you haven't seen before and you are now more knowledgeable. If the owners aren't home, call the number and start asking them questions to understand how you can help. Here are some questions and phrases you can say:

For FSBOs-

- How long have you been trying to sell your property unrepresented?

- What was your main reason for selling it without an agent?

- How many offers have you had?

- Just out of curiosity, where were you planning to move when you sell?

- How many appts have you had in the past week?

- Why are you selling?

- If I could show you how you could NET more money by listing with me would you be interested?

Many FSBOs cooperate with brokers and pay a commission % if you bring them a buyer.

As for expired listings, being the first or second agent calling is vital. Once an expired listing owner has gotten 5-10 calls from agents, they lose interest and patience in discussing much.

For Expireds-

- If you are calling immediately after it has expired you can ask "Are you aware your property is now expired and no longer for sale?"

- I'm sorry your property didn't sell, I'm sure it's very frustrating. Why do you think it didn't sell?

- Your property sounds great, I'm surprised it didn't sell. I've helped many owners just like you sell their property successfully the 2nd time around.

- Are you still interested in selling? If Yes, you can say "I'm confident I can sell your property and I will be in your neighborhood today and would love to take just a few minutes of your time to show you how I can do that for you. Is 4pm good or is 6pm after work better?

2. Door Knocking   FREE

Door knocking can be a scary prospect to some agents. Fear of rejection can come into play, along with not knowing what to say or even if you should leave something behind.

One method to ease your way into this tactic is to use door knocking when promoting your open houses. I suggest knocking on 10 doors to the left of the open house property, 10 doors to the right and 10 doors across the street. You are welcome to do more, but that's a good solid start and great way to get the word out about the open house while lead generating for yourself.

Everyone likes to feel special so why not promote a special "neighbor's preview" open house and do it an hour before your regular open house. Neighbors always like to check out each other's homes and what better way to meet other homeowners than to hold a special hour long open just for them.

A simple script for this would be:

"Hello, my name is Paul Fontaine from Keller Williams Philadelphia, I am holding a special open house today from 12-1pm just for neighbors on the block for 123 Main Street which is for sale. I wanted to invite you (hand them a flyer or invite with info) to be the first to see this home and would love to show you around. I know owners often love to see what other neighbors' houses look like. Who do you know that might be looking to move into our neighborhood?.... Great, just out of curiosity have you ever thought of selling?"...

There are many variations to this simple script, but the main components are:

1. Introducing yourself

2. Inviting them to the open house

3. Handing them the flyer with your contact info

4. Asking for any referrals for buying or selling

5. Repeat at next house

Not that scary, right?

CHALLENGE: At your next open house add door knocking to your promotion schedule and knock on 30 doors prior

to the open.

3. Do at least 3 open houses per week   FREE

Good ol' open houses, agents have a love/hate relationship with this perennial favorite. They are pretty much free of cost and can be done any hour of any day so, for those reasons and more, I will always be a fan of them. Every agent has his or her own method of holding an open house. Some sit on the couch and on their phone while open house attendees are milling around. Some agents greet you at the door and follow you around pointing out specific aspects of the home. Open houses tend not to be a primary way of selling the actual home that is open, but they are good ways to meet potential clients (both buyers and sellers).

I laugh every time I ask an agent how their open house was and they say "it was ok, not great, only 1-2 buyers came and the rest were nosy neighbors" Nosy neighbors are the best! As an agent, who are the people you want to be face to face with on a consistent basis?   Owners! Those neighbors are mostly all owners of homes who may need assistance now or in the future. Plus if they really are "nosy neighbors" they probably speak to a lot of other neighbors and know the scoop on what's happening and who might be looking to sell.

Our goal, as agents, is to always add value to the people we come into contact with so why not print out a sheet of 3-4 other homes for sale in the area with similar price points and give that to open house attendees after they have toured the home? Most open house attendees will not be interested in that particular home so take advantage of being there in person and giving them a handout with valuable information (along with your contact information) can be very beneficial.

Lastly, and most importantly, one of your main goals at an open house is to make a connection with people and obtain their contact information. Giving your contact information is okay, but getting their contact information is GREAT. You want the power to be in your hands, not the other people. You can't follow-up without their contact information and waiting around for them to contact you isn't the way to build your business. Get contact information!

4. Join your neighborhood association or condo board   FREE

Many neighborhoods have a neighborhood association. If yours doesn't, then join another neighborhood's association. Who says you have to live in that exact neighborhood in order to help? I am a huge advocate for giving back to society and this strategy achieves that along with helping you generate quality leads. You have the pleasure of being part of positive changes in your neighborhood, while also connecting with many people, mostly homeowners. People that get involved in neighborhood associations tend to be passionate people who want to make their neighborhood a better place. If they see that you also have similar interests, who do you think they will hire or refer next time real estate assistance is needed?

In the same vein, if you live in a condo or a community, you can join the board or homeowner's association. It's a great way to keep up to date with what's going on and to stay "top of mind" with fellow owners.

5. Join other organizations. FREE

It doesn't particularly matter what type of organization, it can be anything. Whether it's for fun, personal or professional. In my opinion, the best organizations would be ones with a lot of people and also with many opportunities to get to know each other. A lot of my sales come from organizations I am a member of or non-profits where I volunteer. It's a wonderful way to do things you enjoy or help out those in need while also building strong relationships and connections.

You don't need to discuss real estate or act any differently than you usually are with people. If you are spending time with people in those organizations, eventually it comes out that you are a real estate agent and it all flows naturally from there. No need for hard selling or scripting, just the natural progression of getting to know people.

6. Use social media   FREE

One can write an entire book (and people have) regarding real estate marketing and social media. Some of the main ones are Facebook, Instagram and Twitter but there are hundreds and probably thousands of other sites/apps that can be used for purposes of generating leads and building an online presence. Some methods of using social media include:

1. Utilize Facebook's birthday notifications to say happy birthday to all your "Friends"

2. Want to stand out, don't just put the default "Happy Birthday" message. People can get hundreds of those on their birthday. Do a quick video or how about Google what happened on that date and share a quick tidbit with them. You have to put in more effort in order to achieve better results.

3. Using Facebook's Live video function is a great way to add some excitement as everyone loves "live" events. We, as agents, take things for granted and often think everyone knows how it is to attend a home inspection or how it is to view penthouse condos overlooking the city.

4. Take pictures of you and your clients. Posts without photos do not get much response. Share your daily life with everyone and use it for both entertainment and educational purposes. Your "audience" will appreciate it and think of you next time they need any real estate assistance.

5. Join different Facebook groups and communities and

be an active participant in posting and responding.

Most experts say you should post once a day and no more than twice. If you are posting too often, the interest from followers begins to decrease and you will see less "likes" from your posts.   https://blog.hubspot.com/marketing/facebook-post-frequency-benchmarks

7. Act like a buyer or seller. FREE

On a regular basis, once or twice a year, put on your "buyer or seller hat" and pretend you are interested in selling your home or buying a place.   What would you do first?   Many go online and search so why not do the same.   Google "how to buy a home in Austin" or "Sell my condo in Miami" and see what results come up.   Find out what websites are out there connecting agents with clients. Go to any sites that connect agents with clients and sign up. There are new sites popping up each year and many are free to sign up. You tend to have to pay a referral fee for website leads but 65-75% of commission is better than no commission in my world.

8. Create events COST VARIES

Holding events can take a lot of effort at times, but it is one of the best methods of meeting people and building new relationships. Also, creating client appreciation events helps further build your existing relationships. Some ideas for events are:

1. Set up a table at your gym and give away towels or water bottles with your branding. A gym is a great place to make contact with people. Depending on your workout schedule, there's a good chance you see the same people over and over again 2-3 times a week.

2. Fundraising events can be a wonderful way to give back to a worthy cause and also connect with people having similar interests.

3. Create a street or block cleaning event and invite all the neighbors to join. Have a table with some coffee and donuts to entice owners to come out of their houses.

4. Hold a free home buyer or seller seminar at your office. Want to entice people a little more? Hold a seminar at a local bar or restaurant. Partner with a mortgage lender to pay for some of the cost and offer every participant a free drink.

5. The holidays are great times for events. Hire the easter bunny and hold an event at a local park for families to come by. Hire a Santa for your client appreciation party.

Events are a great way to create opportunities to connect with your database. Each event yields at least 8 or more chances to reach out and connect.

Some examples are:

1. Save the date email

2. Sending out an actual invite via postal service is also an option.

3. Call to make sure they received the email or mailing

4. Follow up with a text.

5. Send Facebook event invite

6. A week before the event you can call, email and text again to confirm attendance.

7. At the event, take photos and then you can post them on your page and, if acceptable, tag attendees for more exposure.

8. After the event, call, email and text thanking attendees and letting others know they were missed.

9. Send out direct mail   COST VARIES

I'm always astonished by how little direct mail I get from real estate agents. I probably get less than 5 mailers a year. Studies show on average the response rate for a direct mail piece is approx. 5%. *Data Source: ANA/DMA Response Rate Report 2018*

I don't have any specific studies to quote from, but from my own personal experiences, direct mail tends to work best with the 50+ year old population. Especially 65+. Studies show that the older you are the less time you spend online, so it makes sense that if you are 65+ you will pay more attention to other marketing channels like direct mail.

I've had recipients of my direct mail contact me years later and show me the mail piece that they saved "for when they needed it." This lead generation strategy is definitely not one of the free ones as it can be quite pricey. Since our average profit per sale (aka our commission) is so high per sale it often can be quite profitable to do direct mail. Even with a 1% response rate, if you send out a 2,000 piece mailing quantity, you get two responses and hopefully convert one of those into a sale, you'd do quite well assuming an average commission of $7,000 and a cost of approx. $1,200 using a $.60/piece average for a bulk mailing. (Prices can range from $.50 to $2-$3/piece depending on what you are mailing.

In summary, I would not recommend doing direct mail as one of the first marketing strategies. When you are new, focus on the lead generation strategies that are free or nearly free. Once you get established you can progress into some of the other marketing channels that cost more money.

10.Work on listing leads specifically.　　FREE

In order to become really successful, you'll want to focus more on the listing side of the business. If you are inexperienced, it can be a little easier to get buyer clients vs. seller clients. Most people don't interview numerous buyer agents, but often people interview several seller agents. If you don't have a lot of past sales to discuss with owners, use your office or team stats to lean on for experience. If an owner asks "how much did you sell last year or have you ever sold in this building before?" You can say "my office is #2 in the city and sold over $30 million." or "my team sold a unit on the 20th floor 6 months ago"

By working on listing leads and building your listing business you will increase your overall leads. For every listing you have, you should yield 2 additional buyer leads. Those leads may come from such sources as open houses or for sale sign calls.

SPECIAL BONUS: Want my personal "listing to do checklist" on *How to Sell your Listings in 30 days or less!* email me at Paul@BestPhillyHomes.com

11. Work on referrals to other agents
APPROX 25% REFERRAL FEE

One of my favorite parts of being an agent is the ability to make money so easily when it comes to referrals. By simply giving another agent the name and contact info for a potential buyer or seller, you typically will receive 25% of that agent's commission at the time of closing! I've had years where I've had over 10 referrals for people I knew that were looking to buy in towns or states outside of my area. The typical referral commission I get is around $3,500. It's something many agents, especially new ones forget about and don't focus on enough. Make sure you consistently let everyone you know that if they need any real estate assistance to let you know.

It's an easy script I use when it comes to this strategy. If your seller client mentions something about moving to another state or if a friend says their colleague is leaving the job to start a new one in a different state just say "I have a great agent in (whatever town/city they say they are moving to), do you want their information?" Now there is a good chance I don't know someone personally in that city, but I will immediately go online and research some top agents and make a couple phone calls to get 1-2 good options to give to my client.

12. Work on referrals from other agents FREE

Now that we perfected sending referrals to other agents for fast money, let's concentrate on being the person other agents go to with their referrals!

There are a few strategies with this one:

1. Make sure you continue to add and build your database of agents so you can communicate with them.(more on that in a bit).

2. Send out an email a couple of times a year discussing your referral fee and letting them know you are the best agent for their referral clients.

3. Continue to network at conventions and outside of office trainings.

By the way, I would be negligent if I didn't walk the walk and talk the talk, so this is my formal ask to any agents reading this, if you ever need a great agent in the Philadelphia area... Call Paul!   215-917-2276 or Paul@BestPhillyHomes.com. .

13.   Build and feed your Database   FREE

A database is simply a term used to describe a structured set of information.

This is one of the most effective methods to building your business for any agent, whether brand new or a veteran. Creating, maintaining, growing and communicating with your database should be an ongoing, daily practice. For any agent who says they don't have a database, they are lying.   Do you have a phone?   That's a database.

For our purposes as agents, our databases consist of contact information of leads, clients, etc.   Preferably, first and last name, mailing address, phone number and email address.   If you are more advanced, each contact record could include spouse names, children's names, anniversary or birthdates, pet names, etc.

When I have taught this in a class sometimes agents say "but I don't have a lot of their contact info" and I say "Great! That gives you a reason to contact them" Do you have an email? Then email and say you are updating your database and you are missing their phone #.   Have their phone number, but no email address? What a great reason to call them up to touch base and say you are about to send out a new market update and saw that you were missing their email address. Maybe you have their phone # and email address. Ask for a physical mailing address. Have all 3, how about asking for their birthday or anniversary? Two significant dates that you can use to call contacts or send out celebratory messages to make them feel special.

The National Association of Realtors (NAR) has reported that 78% of buyers and sellers would re-use their agent next time they need real estate assistance but only 24% actually did re-use them! Why? Because agents didn't keep in touch. Years go by and an owner's life changes and they need to sell and they say to themselves, "What was the name of that agent we used to buy the place? Was it Lori or Lisa? Maybe Marci?" If you don't keep in touch, memories fade and you will be lost in the minds of your previously happy clients.

In the world of the Internet, it takes 2.3 seconds for that owner to Google "real estate agent in Boston" and come up with a lot of agents to contact. Some sites will even have them ranked to make the choice easier. Don't get lost in the mind of your past clients. Communicate regularly using your database system. It's really not that hard to send out emails monthly or quarterly to your past clients. Companies like Constant Contact or Mailchimp are just a couple of options for your emailing needs.

As you progress as an agent you will have a lot of past clients, neighbors, friends in your database. I've gone a step further and segmented a group of my top 100 supporters. I thought of a catchy name "VIP group" which stands for Very Important to Paul! This is the group I communicate with the most and give top level attention. Sometimes I offer free gifts to the first 10 that reply to an email (I always request they meet me to receive the gift so I am able to get some important one-on-one time with them). Take time to think about what is of interest to your clients and database. Once you figure that out, "feed" the people in your database those things that add value and interest them.

CHALLENGE: Add 5 people to your database today. It can be friends, neighbors, past clients, leads, members of your church, work associates, etc. Don't have their phone number, then email and ask them for it. Don't have their email, then call them and ask. Don't have either, send a message on Facebook.

14. Make contact with people. FREE

Real estate is a contact sport. Tying in with the previous section, making contact with people is crucial to running a successful business. Knowing your numbers starts with contacts. You need a certain # of contacts to turn into qualified leads. Some of those leads then turn into clients and ultimately those clients turn into closed sales. It all starts with contacts. You must make contact with people. " But who do I contact?" say some agents. My answer is anyone. Start with the people you know the best and move forward from there. Some methods of making contact are:

1. Phone calls

2. Text messages

3. Emails

4. Sending direct mail

5. Door knocking

6. Open Houses

7. Attending networking events

8. Attending neighborhood or condo association meetings

9. Social media messaging

10. Walking into businesses.

We will discuss some of these in more detail in this book. The next tactic we discuss will be about phone calls and that's one place to start.

15. Make Phone calls   FREE BUT CAN VARY

This can be a free strategy or you can pay a company to send you contact names, phone numbers and emails of FSBOs or Expired listings.   Making phone calls is one of the best ways to have effective communication with owners looking to sell. This is not an effort that can be done half-heartedly.   You can't call 3 numbers and say, "I tried and no one was home" or "I called and 2 hung up on me and 1 was the wrong number. Calling doesn't work." Just like most things; it's a numbers game.

Statistics vary, but in general you have to call approximately 10 people to get 1 person on the phone for a conversation. And you need anywhere from 5-8 conversations to book an appointment for selling or buying.   Doing that math on those statistics means you need to make on average around 65 phone calls to get an appointment!

Studies show the best times to call are 8-9am and 4-6pm. Worst time to call is 12-2pm. If they don't answer on the first call, do not leave a message. Try them back in a half hour. Sometimes you'll get a callback sooner than that from a curious caller wondering who called and didn't leave a message.

This is where your passion and drive and your WHY comes into play.   You will deal with some rejection and possibly some negative comments when you make phone calls.   Try not to let it affect you or take it personally. Everyone has his or her own life going on and you don't know what is driving the response. Remind yourself that you are there to add value and to help. If they don't want your assistance right now, move on. As I like to say, "Next!"

Phone calls should also be made to your past clients and those that know you well. Following up on a market update you sent them or calling on their birthdays are two good reasons to touch base. Keep it short and keep it about them. Adding in a phone call to your marketing schedule is always worthwhile whenever you send out an email or direct mail piece. Just a simple "Hey, just touching base to make sure you received the market update. Did you have any questions?" will suffice. Try to catch them live but if after a couple of no answer attempts, at least you can leave a message so they hear your voice.

16. Send out emails   FREE

As discussed previously, having a database is essential. CRMs (Customer Relationship Management) systems aren't too expensive and can be used to send out professional looking emails with photos and links to your database. A good CRM will keep track of what emails you sent, what the open rate was, how many clicks you got for your links and what % of emails bounced back. When emails bounce back it can be for a number of reasons, but most likely they have changed their address or are no longer at that email so you are sending an email to no one and you should either delete that information or a much better option is to research and find the correct information for that person so you can now send them communication.

It's important to classify your database into different groups depending on their current real estate status. An example of recommended groups would be buyer leads, seller leads, past clients, neighbors, family, church, etc. Once they are grouped, you will send out emails to keep in contact with clients, leads, friends and neighbors with content that is geared specifically toward them.

17. Send texts.   FREE

Often when I call someone who doesn't answer, especially if it's for lead generation, I send them a text.   You'll be surprised how often you will get a reply to your text seconds after not getting an answer from your call. Some people can't talk at that moment but are able to text. Some just don't like to talk on the phone or answer phones.

You can use text message marketing also. Text messages have a 98% open rate, which far outshines any other form of communication such as email, phone calls or direct mail. DialMyCalls is one company that does text automation. Just like many modes of communication, you have to be careful and make sure people getting your texts have given you some type of permission to receive them.

18. Create videos   MOSTLY FREE

Within 2 months of creating videos, I received my first lead. This person wrote in a manner as if he knew me. He laid out all of his pertinent information and said he wanted help buying a place because he was relocating. What a refreshing email to receive when someone is open and willing to give you all of their contact information and has already decided they want to work with you!

You can create videos on your iPhone and Android or you can spend money to have a professional do your videos. In general, I'm still in the mindset that phone videos are acceptable and effective for most endeavors. Videos help people get to know you better and also it's an opportunity to put a face with a name. Some top agents who use video say that often they go to listing appointments with someone they consider a stranger, but that person acts like they've known them for years since they see their videos so often.

YouTube has over 1.5 billion monthly active users watching up to 1 hour of video so there's a good chance your clients are on it also. Youtube is one of the largest search engines just like Google. Creating a YouTube channel is free. There are entire books on using video for real estate and how to use search terms, titles and tags to make it the most effective.

Some good ideas for videos are:

1. client testimonials

2. neighborhood info

3. open house teaser

4. relocation info on your city

5. agent profile

6. team features

7. seller and buyer presentations

8. Thank you for Appt or business

One important tip: keep it short. Depending on what type of video you are doing, some shouldn't be longer than 30 seconds; most should never be more than 2-4 minutes. On average, only 37% of viewers watch a video until the very end so don't keep the most exciting content until the bitter end!

CHALLENGE: *Commit to doing one video this month. There's a great course I took to learn almost everything I know. Here is a link to learn more and to sign up if you'd like.*

https://www.youtubeforagentscourse.com/courses/youtube-for-agents?ref=4cb06e

Let this be your first step towards making progress on this lead generation tool.

If you haven't already visited, for different ideas, check out my YouTube channel. youtube.com/c/paulfontainerealtor.

19. Develop a personal brochure   COST VARIES

If you are working hard and doing everything in this book to build your business, you will find that you need a general handout or brochure to give to people. You can use it for door knocking, FSBOs or expireds mailings, listing presentations, etc.   Make sure you add some nice color photos of you, or your team, along with some visuals or eye-catching graphics. Again keep it simple. I wouldn't be too specific with things because hopefully it can be generic enough for you to use for many years.

Adding something personal is always a good touch. People do business with agents that they like and trust and sharing parts of your life helps them get to know you and start building trust. There are tons of companies and websites you can go to in order to create a brochure and they aren't super expensive. Usually you can get 250 brochures for less than $100 and some companies help design it for you.

20. Sign up for floor time   FREE

When I first began in 2003, I was called "The Floor King" 90% of the sales in my first year were from sitting at our office's front desk answering incoming phone calls aka Floor time. I think floor time was a little more fruitful back then. These days, with the Internet and apps, there are less people calling phone numbers on for sale signs. I still think agents should do it, especially newer ones.   Many offices offer a way to sign up for a shift or two each month in order to get any leads that call in. Why not utilize the opportunity to accept any free leads coming in?

21. Ask for referrals consistently   FREE

Anytime is a good time to ask for referrals, but asking at high points of a client's transaction such as closings or when the property goes into escrow or under agreement, can be the most productive. My advice is to start early on, even at your first meeting.   Let them know your business is built on referrals and if they enjoy working with you to please let you know of anyone they know looking to buy or sell real estate.

I always like to say to my favorite clients "I love working with you and you probably hang around other people that are just like you. I'd love to help them too, do you know of anyone looking to buy or sell?"

In addition to asking clients, it is important to ask as many people as you can on a consistent basis. Some examples are:

- Other parents in your child's play group

- Members of your church or synagogue

- Contractors that are on your recommended contractor list

- Neighbors

Do your best to tie the "ask" into your genuine conversations. After discussing important aspects of the person's life such as family, work and future fun plans say "Just curious, who do you know that may be looking to buy or sell?" It's always good to keep it as an open-ended question rather than "Do you know anyone looking to buy or sell?" The answer to that will most always be "no."

I always send a hand-written thank you card with a gift card to anyone that gives me a referral. I don't wait to see if the referral is "good" or if it closes. I want to reward the behavior which is to send me referrals. They can't control if that person buys or sells. Last, but not least, when someone sends you a referral, keep them in the loop regarding any updates. If you meet with that referral, send a quick text or email stating "Thank you again for referring Sam to me. I met with him today and had a great conversation. We are planning on seeing a few properties for sale next week." People appreciate being appreciated and also good, effective communication is always a great policy.

22. Create a recommended vendor/contractor list. FREE

My list of contractors is a hot commodity in my sphere of influence. I recommend that you generate a list, as quickly as possible, of reliable, talented contractors (at times more challenging than you'd think). Clients (and everyone to be honest) are often looking for a good "handyman" or plumber or hardwood floor installer. What better way to add value than to have a list of names and contact info you can send to them.

Don't know any contractors? Here are some ways to create an effective contractor list:

1. Find them. Go and meet business owners and contractors by either walking into their business or calling them to schedule a quick meetup.

2. Ask around for recommendations. Post on social media requesting advice on who friends have worked with for their homes. Not only is this exercise good for adding value to your clients, but it also makes networking connections with those actual contractors and businesses.

3. Hire them. They will be more prone to give out your name to any of their clients looking for real estate assistance.

4. Make sure you cull through the list annually to weed out any bad numbers, businesses no longer around or delete contractors you get bad reviews about from clients who used them. There's always risk in giving recommendations. No matter how hard you try to send the best contractors you will always hear about some bad experiences so be prepared.

Quick tip: I always make sure my clients give my name when they call those contractors so they know I'm sending them business.

23. Ask other agents to "sit" their open houses
FREE

New to the business or been around and don't have many listings? Leverage your office and ask around to find out who has too many listings to handle personally and see if you can "sit" some of their open houses (aka the agent who actually is at the open house and conducts it). Hopefully your office is like mine and has many successful agents/teams who have more listings than they can manage in terms of sitting open houses. Typically if you do a good job, those agents will come back to you weekly asking if you are available to sit their open houses. Some successful agents have made holding effective open houses their top lead generating system. Show the other agents you have that passion and fire to succeed and get out there and ask around!

24. Focus on the people closest to you first.
FREE

When you are first starting out, and as a reminder to those who have been an agent for a while, prioritize communicating with the people that know you best. Family, friends, work associates, fellow church members are all examples of groups you should be focusing on first. Only after you have fully communicated and followed-up with your priority group should you move onto the next tier of people who may be acquaintances or friends of friends. After that you can work on connecting with those who don't know you at all.

Sometimes people feel a bit uncomfortable reaching out to those they are closest with because they don't want to "bother" them. Our job as an agent is to help people by adding value and educating them on, probably, their biggest financial decision of their lives. We aren't "bothering" them if we are connecting with them and letting them know we are available to help if they need any real estate assistance.

25.   Find your "farm"   FREE

The final lead generation tool we'll discuss is "farming." In the beginning of Section 2 of this book, I discussed finding a niche. This segment is a continuation of that concept. In real estate, a "farm" is an area you decide to focus on for business.

When we were discussing home turnover rate, usually a 7% turnover rate or higher is a good standard to look at for this analysis. Obviously the higher the turnover rate the more opportunities you will have to list properties in that area.

In addition to analyzing home turnover rates, it's advantageous to research agents to rank them and see what % of business the top 5 agents have in that area (if you don't know how to do this call your local Multiple Listing Service

MLS service). In my MLS, you can do a simple search by listing agent or if you don't have that option, do a search by area and create your own spreadsheet counting up the number of listings each agent has in that area. If one agent has 40% of the market, it doesn't mean you shouldn't focus on that area but it will certainly make it a bit more challenging. The areas that don't have one or two dominant players (30% or more) can be more conducive to becoming the #1 agent for those residents.

BONUS SECTION

I hope you found this book enriching and have already begun implementing some of these strategies and challenges.   If you've made it to this point in the book, congratulations! It shows you have that drive and passion to succeed.

The following are some bonus tips and strategies for you as you continue on your journey to Be The Exception!

How about if you...

- Create a market update each month or quarter and email to neighbors, clients and friends

- Buy a bunch of books and offer to give clients or others a real estate investing book to read. Gather the recipients names and contact info and follow-up with them in a few weeks to see how they are enjoying the book.

- Belong to a gym? Talk to the gym manager, maybe you can sponsor a fitness class. Or how about print a few t-shirts with your name and catchy slogan and wear it to workout. It's free advertising and you don't even have to say a word.

- Make sure you utilize your email signature as much as possible. Make an automated signature that goes on each email you send. In the signature put your name, phone numbers, website, Facebook URL, Instagram handle.

- In marketing, always add a P.S. to letters or emails, etc. Studies show people will read the headlines, first sentence and P.S. before the rest.

- Partner with your mortgage lenders, title companies or insurance agents to co-market anything. Typically these partners will pay for a portion of the marketing costs.

- One good app you can download that's neighborhood specific is Nextdoor. It's a great way to connect with your neighbors and know what's going on in your area.

- Get client reviews. Many buyers and sellers go online to read reviews when deciding which agent to represent them. There are many sites where reviews can be written such as google.com, yelp.com, zillow.com, facebook.com etc. Ask clients to write you a quick review and follow-up if you don't hear back from them the first time you ask.

- Wear your real estate agent name tag wherever you go. I love marketing strategies that take little to no effort. Just put it on in the morning and you'll be surprised how often the topic of real estate will come up.

- Want to compare your listing results with the average agent in your area? For your business, calculate your average days on the market for your listings and also the % between list price and sell price. To get average days on the market, add up the number of days on the market for all of your closed listings and divide by the number of closings. To get a % list to sell price, add up the original listing price of all of your listings then add up to actual sold price for those same listings. Now divide the total sold price by total list price. Assuming your figures are better than your competition, these are two key figures to relay to potential sellers. (You want a lower average days on the market and a higher % list to sold).

Want more great info? Check out BestPhillyHomes.com

Have a great marketing idea that I haven't mentioned? I'd love to hear about it. Drop me an email and send me your ideas and it could be added to the next edition of this book with credits to you! Paul@BestPhillyHomes.com.

PAUL FONTAINE

CHALLENGES' SUMMARY

CHALLENGE: What do you love doing? What brings you the most joy? For example, do you feel most alive when you are helping others? Does baking excite you? Also, what are the things you never want to experience or feel? Maybe you grew up seeing your single mother struggle to make ends meet and you never want her to struggle again. Or you will never forget the embarrassment of going to school with old or dirty clothes because your parents couldn't afford to buy you new ones.

CHALLENGE: Why do you NEED to be a successful real estate agent? Before reading on, write down your WHY. No, seriously, stop reading and spend 15-30+ minutes thinking, writing down, brainstorming, digging deep and asking the important "whys?" to get to your emotional trigger.

CHALLENGE: When you go to YouTube.com to check out my channel, take the first step and create your own channel. You will first need a gmail email account (go to gmail.com). Once you have a gmail address, you can then go to that account and click on YouTube and create an account. That is the first step to having your own YouTube Channel!

CHALLENGE: Ask yourself "Am I being consistent with the most important aspects of my business?" Take a step back from yourself for a moment and act as if you were reviewing someone else's day to day activities. Do you see a consistent pattern each day regarding key elements of sustaining a successful business?

CHALLENGE: Write down 5-10 affirmations and read them aloud each morning and/or evening. Make sure you read them aloud. There's something about saying them and hearing the words that are more powerful than reading silently. While you are at it, tape those affirmations in your office or next to your bathroom mirror to see them numerous times a day.

CHALLENGE: Search for motivational songs, speeches, podcasts or albums and download a few of your favorites.

CHALLENGE: Find an accountability buddy and make them a promise that you will call them once a day or week (whatever you choose) to give an update on your goals and initiatives.

CHALLENGE: If you have not set and written down your goals, take a day or two this week and work on it. To keep *it simple, decide on your goal for:*

- Number of appointments per year (divide by 52 to get a weekly goal)

- Number of signed buyer and seller client contracts per year

- Number of settlements (broken out between # of buyers and sellers)

- Estimate average sales price of each settlement

- Total sales dollar volume goal for the year (ave sales price * number of settlements)

CHALLENGE: Write down your top 5 things you'd like to accomplish today, then prioritize them and get started on #1.

CHALLENGE: Write out one hand-written note today. It can be to anyone. Don't overthink it, just sit down and begin. A few days later when you get a call or text from that person saying how sweet it was to get your card, you'll be glad you did it!

CHALLENGE: Schedule 5 appointments this week to view some homes you haven't seen in an area you want to specialize in or a new area you aren't familiar with yet.

CHALLENGE: I recommend doing this simple analysis for numerous other neighborhoods and communities to get 5-10 different data points for you to see if there is a void you can fill and become the real estate "king or queen" for that high turnover area.

CHALLENGE: Choose one of the books listed, purchase it and read Chapter a chapter each day.

CHALLENGE: Research upcoming seminars, conferences or webinars in your company and sign up for one this week.

CHALLENGE: Tell at least 1 new person each day that you are in real estate and ask them how you can help.

CHALLENGE: Make a formal, written goal to purchase a property within the next year. Either a primary residence or an investment property.

CHALLENGE: Do you know what your expenses are each month? If not, go through bills, receipts and bank statements and create a spreadsheet of all your expenses for the past month. I use Reprophet.com to track all of my expenses.

CHALLENGE: Brainstorm and write down 3-5 value add items you could give to leads or clients. Some examples are market updates, refinance information, home selling tips, contractor recommendation lists, etc.

CHALLENGE: Think about who you know that would be a good mentor. Who do you admire? Who have you learned from previously?   Can't think of anyone? Then think about where you could go in order to find someone that could be helpful?   Local real estate organization? Chamber of commerce? Your alma mater?

CHALLENGE: Never taken the DISC personality test? Go to discpersonalitytesting.com to take a free DISC test.

CHALLENGE: Choose a specific area of business you want to practice with such as listing presentations, buyer presentations, objection handling or lead conversion. If you are a Keller Williams agent there are plenty of scripts available to study and practice. If your company doesn't offer that, I would recommend searching online for "realtor scripts" or check out tomferry.com or theclose.com.

CHALLENGE: At your next open house add door knocking to your promotion schedule and knock on 30 doors prior to the open.

CHALLENGE: Add 5 people to your database today. It can be friends, neighbors, past clients, leads, members of your church, work associates, etc.   Don't have their phone number, then email and ask them for it. Don't have their email, then call them and ask. Don't have either, send a message on Facebook.

CHALLENGE: Commit to doing one video this month. There's a great course I took to learn almost everything I *know.   Here is a link to learn more and to sign up if you'd like.*

MEET THE AUTHOR

Dear reader,

I sincerely appreciate you reading **How to Be a Successful Real Estate Agent** using Kindle, Print and Audio Book. I hope the strategies and tips were useful and that you will use them consistently to achieve your goals. *If you have enjoyed this book, please consider being kind enough to leave a review on Amazon.* Tap this link and scroll down to where it says, "want to leave a review."

You can find me at: facebook.com/PaulLouisFontaine.

Come check out my YouTube channel with tons of real estate videos. youtube.com/c/PaulFontaineRealtor.

My contact information: Paul Fontaine. Keller Williams Philadelphia 1619 Walnut St 5th flr, Phila, PA 19103. paul@BestPhillyHomes.com. 215-627-3500 office. 215-917-2276 mobile.

Want more information on Keller Williams Realty? Looking for an agency to join or move to? I'd love to answer your questions. Email or Call Paul!

Special Thanks to

David Fontaine for Editing Expertise

Made in the USA
Las Vegas, NV
28 October 2023

79875704R00069